A <u>QUICK</u> Guide to Writing and Publishing Your Book...

MELVINA L. CARPENTER

Dedication...

This book is dedicated to my Lord and savior Jesus Christ who has laid his hands upon me and instilled knowledge, wisdom and understanding to write! He has equipped me with this gift and I am eternally grateful. I empathize with the writer of Psalms 45:1b, where he states, *"My heart is inditing a good matter: I speak of the things which I have made touching the king: my tongue is the pen of a ready writer."* (KJV)

To my parents, my husband, our children, my siblings and my friends, thank you for believing in me and pushing me to write! I love you all dearly.

Table of Contents

Chapter 1...
"Prompting to Write"

In 2007, I published my first novel, "Single, Pregnant and Preaching". If someone had told me a few years prior that I would be an author I would have laughed in their face! However, my college professor, the late Dr. Roosevelt Ratliff, Jr of Claflin University went against the grain and told me what I should be doing. The year 2005 is where the journey began.

While grading my thesis paper in preparation for my bachelor's degree, Dr. Ratliff called me into his office and said two sentences that has forever changed my world! He said to me, "You write very well. Have you considered writing a book?" I still remember the look of confusion on my face as he spoke those unfamiliar words to me. I felt important, secure, and intelligent.

Those words were never spoken to me before. My parents always encouraged me that I could be whomever I wanted to be. However, none of my teachers or professors ever pushed me in a specific direction prior to this encounter with Dr. Ratliff.

His words resounded in my ear! I could not fathom the idea that a college professor saw something in me that no one pointed out to me before! The next thing on my agenda was to decide if what he was telling me was the truth, or if I should take the compliment and keep it moving.

Well, as you can see, I decided to evaluate what he said and see what would become of it. I looked over my previous grades for all my classes that involved writing. I was reminded that my scores were very high. I was also reminded of how I rolled my eyes and sulked at the thought of writing yet another paper. However, I loved and still love reading. I thought about the types of books that I enjoyed and questioned if I could write something similar to what I read. Terry McMillian, Omar Tyree, Bishop T.D. Jakes, Mary Monroe, and Maya Angelou were a few authors who came to mind that I wouldn't dare compare myself to. Furthermore, I questioned my skills, my motivation and determination. I then typed my first paragraph and found that I fell in love with something new that was in my presence all along.

Chapter 2...
"Is this Your Assignment?"

This leads me to my first point with you. As the reader, the first thing that you must ask yourself is…"Is this MY assignment"? Is writing your assignment? Is it really something that you could see yourself doing, often? Do you have something that you'd like to talk about just once and then you'd like to never pick up a pen or click keys on a laptop again? Is it something that awakens you from your sleep at night and steals your focus during the day because it's all that you can think about? Are you mentally snatched away from conversations with peers because while they are speaking you are daydreaming about the next paragraph of your book? While contemplating one title, does another title creep into to your mind? If you said yes to any of these questions then I would say, go for it. However, the decision to begin writing is merely the beginning. Here are a few questions that I believe need to be answered before the pen touches the paper.

What types of books do you enjoy reading? Who are your favorite authors? Which titles of those authors speak to you the most and why? Can you see yourself, adding a paragraph to those authors books or changing something about it? I would admonish you to take a moment and answer these questions.

While you answer the above questions, thinking about the following questions. What types of books would you like to write? There is a plethora of subjects to be discussed. Where do you fit in? Who is your audience? Who are you trying to reach, influence or entertain? Are you speaking to teenagers, toddlers, adults, Christians, Non-Christians, a specific gender, or race of people? Will your book be a self-help book, a love novel, fiction or nonfiction?

In addition, here are a few more paramount questions to ask yourselves before you write the first word. What's your purpose for writing? Do you want to write because you're very creative and you'd like to express yourself on paper? Are you writing to be recognized as a best- selling author and become famous? Is writing something that's simply on your bucket list?

Once you've answered these questions then we can move forward. If writing truly is your passion, you'll never get it out of your system until you get it done. You'll never finish if you never start. I'd like to share a little bit more about my journey of writing my first five books.

Chapter 3...
"Trials of the first Novel"

After acknowledging what was spoken to me regarding my gifts and talents, I thought about what I would write. I started several books, romance novels, sermons, and children's books, to say the least. However, none of those books spoke to my heart like "Single, Pregnant and Preaching." Because my focus was on Christian readers who are familiar with the moral struggles of sex before marriage; I wanted to shed light on the issue of fornication among single people in the church. I realized that I wanted to speak to single women and people who are church affiants. I wanted Pastor's to know how single people feel and I wanted single people to know that I empathized with them as well.

Two years later, Single, Pregnant and Preaching was sitting in my hands! I was thrilled. The process wasn't easy. There were times that I felt discouraged. There were times that I wanted to trash the entire manuscript. Nevertheless, I continued writing. Once my manuscript was finished, I searched for a publishing company. I had very little computer skills beyond Microsoft office suite. Therefore, I needed everything done from my cover design, book format and layout, editing services and so much more. After searching relentlessly, on the world wide wed, I settled on a company that I will refrain from mentioning in this book. They promised me the bells and whistles. I just knew I would make the best seller's list! They promised me that I would have my book in all major book stores. What they meant was my book would be available online in all major bookstores!

They promised me one hundred printed copies of my book, bookmarks, postcards, flyers and other items for my media kit and press release. They sent me these items to market my book. However, when their website said that they offered marketing services, I thought this was included in the $1500.00 that I paid them. I immediately envisioned my photo on the wall of Barnes and Noble. Sadly, it hasn't happened yet. My royalties guaranteed me forty percent of the sale while they gained seventy percent. I was brand new at this writing thing, so I thought that this price point and valuation was ok. I just wanted to meet Oprah. I'll take ten percent; to their ninety percent if I can meet Oprah! How naïve was I?

Interestingly enough, seven years later, my book sales were only accounted for by the sales that I personally inquired or that family and friends sent to me. I took credit card payments from people and ordered the books from amazon myself and had them delivered to the customer's mailing address. Therefore, I knew the sales were real. Yet, in ninety days which is when I should have received my royalty check, I received less than $10.00 for a book that costs $16.00 each. I had accumulated sales of at least one thousand books throughout this seven-year time span, but I only earned approximately $150.00.

I called this publishing company to express my grief. They had no record of the sales from amazon. I had to print my receipts from amazon and fax them to this company for them to mail my royalties to me. It was very disheartening, and I wanted to quit. In fact, I did quit. I said I would never publish another book again!

However, that didn't hold true. In 2015, I hired a lawyer. The lawyer expressed to me that If I wasn't losing thousands or millions of dollars to count my losses and begin again. That's exactly what I did. I called the publishing company to notify them of my upcoming cancellation, confirmed that my contract had ended, wrote them a letter and cancelled my title with them along with all future sales. I revamped my cover, further edited my book and published it again. I became my own publisher! I published my book, but I utilized a printing company called Createspace.com, which is pretty well known.

Chapter 4...
"Publishing Companies vs. Printing Companies"

Let's pause for a moment to define publishing versus printing companies in the simplest terms possible. A publishing company does all the leg work for you. You give specifics on the color of the cover, color of the pages, size of the book, where you'd like your author photo to be placed, etc. However, the publishing company follows your orders as far as what your book looks like. They however, oversee your royalties. They also take part ownership of your manuscript. They will send you promotional items and set your book up for sales on amazon.com, barnesandnoble.com, booksamillion.com, etc. This may vary per company. They will also print copies of your book for you as well and send it to you in bulk. The number of books that they send you will also vary based on the company. Author house, xulonpress, and quill-house are a few of the publishers that will show up if you search for a publishing company as a first-time author. You are still labeled as an Indie Author or self-published but you're under a contract.

However, major publishing companies such as Harper Collins, Random House and Penguin Books takes time and money to reach. These companies are what we all are striving for. You will be under a contract, but your royalties will be much greater. In these cases, your books will reach the shelves of major bookstores and not just online sales. This will increase your chances of becoming a best-selling author. Your manuscript must be sent to them and approved. If they like it, they'll contact you to proceed. This is what we are all praying for.

On the otherhand, a printing company can do all the work for you but you will pay them a fee. You can do the work yourself, upload it to their site and when your book is ordered, they simply print it for you. They will print it for you regardless of where it's ordered from, i.e., amazon, kindle direct publishing, Barnes and Nobles, Books a Million, etc. However, *you* are the publisher. You are an Indie Author, but *you* are in control! You will set your price and your royalties. You can remove your book from online services for any reason at any time and re-establish it as well. Companies such as CreateSpace, Ingram sparks, lulu, amazon and kindle direct publishing, will afford you such privileges.

Chapter 5...
"Companies & Tools that I Utilized"

*Disclaimer: I'm not endorsing; I'm just sharing my story.

As stated earlier, I utilized CreateSpace. I started with Ingram spark but CreateSpace was more user friendly for me. Each person's scenario will be different. You will have to find what works for you. Eventually, I revised "Single, Pregnant and Preaching" in 2015 and put it on the market once more. It took off in a major way and my platform began. Within the same year, I published "Don't Tease the Dog." This book met the eyes of many pet lovers and children all over the world as well. Over the next three years, I wrote and published, "Ungrateful Johnny at Christmas", 30 Days of Prayer and Declarations for Your Pastor" and "Don't Tease Me About My Hair!"

It was during this time that I was constantly asked the same questions: "How did I write my books and who did I use to publish it?" This is the reason for this book. I am by no means am I an expert in this area and I am still striving to reach my goal of becoming a best-selling author. However, with my inbox being filled with questions from various people and types of acquaintances, I gathered in my mind to put the answers in book format. Simply put, these answers may be known by some, but they are certainly not known by all. This is my way of sharing 'How I wrote my books!'

What are you writing about? Don't share your ideas or titles until you have copywritten them. While writing you will have many drafts before the product is complete. Keep your drafts because you'll gather, cut, copy and paste information between all of them! As a writer, you will write on any and everything. My next sentence might be on a sticky note. I might text myself my next paragraph by speaking into my phone! Book titles emerge from books that I'm currently writing. Everything has the potential of being a book to an author. Once you've published your first book, it becomes addictive. Publishing another seems as natural as speaking to your closest friend. Writing becomes your friend. When it does, you will believe that your audience has a need to read your thoughts! What you have to say matters and you are the only one who can produce it! No one can say what you have to say the way that you would say it. If you feel as if I'm talking to you and you're screaming, "yes, that's me", then start writing. If you've laid this book down to take a deep breath because of what you just read because I am speaking to your soul, then start writing.

As previously mentioned, I utilized the printing services of CreateSpace. However, before posting anything to CreateSpace, I had to put the book together for their approval. After saving my work in my email, flash drive and on my personal computer. I proceeded to have my work edited by a trustworthy source. Once it was edited and corrected, I had my work copyrighted at uscopyright.gov. Because the work is sent to the copyright office online and I knew that I hadn't plagiarized anything, I was confident in my upcoming receipt of my letter of copyright.

I then reached out to online sources such as fiverr.com for all my leg work. They have sources on this site for every portion of your book being put together. I hired someone for my cover, my book formatting and layout, illustrations, etc. It is literally a one-stop shop for all your needs regarding your book. For my adult books however, I utilized Istockphoto.com for my book cover and sent it to fiverr.com to prepare my book for CreateSpace.

Once everything that I needed has been accomplished, including preparing my book for print and eBook versions, I uploaded it to createspace.com You will need an isbn (International Standard Book Number) for your book. It's like a social security number for your book. It is one of the most important things that you will need to focus on. This determines where your book can and cannot be sold. CreateSpace has an in-depth breakdown on their page of the differences between their isbn numbers and its benefits. This subject alone would produce another book! You will have to make this decision during your uploading process. Isbns may be purchased at bowker.com or you may utilize free services based on what you want. Please keep in mind that bowker.com is the official isbn purchasing source. Be careful of third parties.

CreateSpace will usher you through the entire process of uploading your book with just a few click of the buttons on your keyboard or desktop computer. Once you've uploaded it and added your description, prices etc., you will receive a letter via email regarding their approval or rejection of the format of your book. If it is rejected, they will tell you what you need to adjust. If it is approved, you will need to purchase a paperback version of your book to give it your final approval. Once you receive it and it meets your standards, you will log onto CreateSpace and complete the process for distribution. CreateSpace will then lead you into the Kindle Direct Publishing process if you'd like to add an eBook version of your book as well. The process will be simpler with your eBook because the file that CreateSpace has received will be used for your eBook as well. The person that you choose on fiverr.com should have created your file for CreateSpace and KDP (Kindle Direct Publishing). Follow the same steps with KDP and just like that, within their allotted time span, your book is officially ready for purchase.

One additional thing that I'd like to mention is children's books. I've published three and I'm contemplating writing a series soon. I'm hesitant, however, because children's books are more difficult to publish in my opinion. I feel this way because once you've written the book and done everything stated above, you must hire an illustrator. Illustrators are expensive! When adding illustrations within children's books, you're basically rewriting the book all over again. This time, with more detail. Your illustrations must line up with your manuscript. For example, Susie can't be wearing an orange blouse in the illustration and the day is cloudy but she's wearing a blue blouse in the manuscript and the day is sunny. What does her hair look like? What's her facial expression? Who else is in the illustration? What are they doing? The questions for illustrations are endless. If you are blessed to find an illustrator who will read your work and bring the illustrations to life for you then you better pay them well. Most illustrators that I have come upon will not be this gracious. I am certainly not trying to deter you from writing children's books. I simply want you to be mindful that it's not as easy as it looks. This all goes back to my topic from the beginning. If you don't want to do the leg work, then hire a publishing company. If you're willing and have the time, then a printing company might be the way you should go. No once can decide that for you, but you.

I'd also like to make you aware that you will never reach best seller status by selling books out of your trunk or garage. You will only reach this goal by consumers purchasing your books from retailers, i.e., Books a Million, Barnes and Noble and Amazon to name a few.

Chapter 6...
"The Do's and Don'ts of this Artistry"

Writing is an art! You are painting the pictures of your mind by gathering them into words and placing them on paper. As an author, you are an artist! However, here are some do's and don'ts of this artistry. Let's pause for a moment to discuss them.

1. Never share your upcoming title unless it's copywritten.

2. Never edit your own book! You need another pair of eyes to edit your book regardless of your feeling. You will need to hire a comprehensive editor to cover all aspects of editing your book to include but not limited to: developmental editing, line editing, copy editing and proofreading.

3. Remember that there are no rules regarding how many words a paragraph contains or how many paragraphs a chapter contains. Once you've made your point, another paragraph or chapter is necessary. Don't make it too short or too long. Simply make your point and move on. For example, in this book, I am quick and to the point to assist my reader. However, in my love novels, I am more detailed to give my readers a

picturesque or descriptive view of what I am describing in written language.

4. Choose a cover that will be eye catching and will capture consumers when browsing online sites or shelves in stores.

5. Have a professional headshot for your author's photo. I know your family or friend's phone takes nice pictures, but have it done professionally.

6. Read the biography of other authors to gain ideas of how to write yours.

7. Write several "about the book" paragraphs. Think about how you respond when someone ask what your book it about. This is what you want to write. Your cover and the "about the book" section is what sells your book. Make sure that it convinces the reader to make the purchase.

8. Always list your contact information in the back of your book. This does not include your personal telephone numbers. Instead it includes your email address, website, and social media sites.

9. Your email, website, and social media sites should all have the same name. For example, my email address is melvina.carpenter@yahoo.com. My website, Facebook, Instagram and twitter handles are Melvina Carpenter's Books. You want your contact information to be relevant to who you are and your brand. It needs to remain the same so

that your followers will always be able to reach you. Don't use the name of your spouse, current job, etc. Things change, and people go away. Use what is memorable to your readers and followers.

10. Upon creating business pages on social media sites, remember to keep it about your book! Remember what your advertising, which is your work, and not yourself. It's ok to post pictures of yourself every now and then but your pages should be primarily about your books.

11. Create and keep business cards with you.

12. Take a writing class. Educating yourself on your craft is essential to your success.

13. Do your research regarding your book title, the printing or publishing company that you choose and the need for what you are writing. Create a plan and stick to it.

Once your book is written, you can take a deep breath and relish in your accomplishment. However, don't get too comfortable because now the real work begins, Marketing! However, you've come this far so you can certainly sell what you've labored to put together. Stay positive and don't procrastinate.

I hope that this book has been of some help to you. Feel free to visit the websites stated above. I am by no means endorsing one over another, I am simply sharing my story and what works for me! I wish you much success! Happy writing to you!

"Please note that this is my story. Since publishing my books and writing this book, Createspace and Kindle Direct Publishing have merged. You may visit kindledirectpublishing.com and they will do everything that createspace has previously done for me."

Special thanks to my readers...

Thank you so much for your support and purchase of one or more of my books. I hope that you enjoyed it! Please remember to write a review and tell others about me as well. I wanted to make you aware of my other titles which include but are not limited to:

"Single, Pregnant and Preaching"
https://www.amazon.com/dp/0692486798/ref=cm_sw_em_r_mt_dp_U__ehV6BbMFK6NGP

"30 Days of Prayer and Declarations of Your Pastor"
https://www.amazon.com/dp/1533265992/ref=cm_sw_em_r_mt_dp_U__oiV6BbA83K5XF

"Don't Tease the Dog"
https://www.amazon.com/dp/0692537996/ref=cm_sw_em_r_mt_dp_U__MiV6BbWF63YTV

"Ungrateful Johnny at Christmas"
https://www.amazon.com/dp/1522823565/ref=cm_sw_em_r_mt_dp_U__BmV6Bb0Q26NVT

"Don't Tease Me About My Hair"
https://www.amazon.com/dp/1978292031/ref=cm_sw_em_r_mt_dp_U__hnV6BbF2M1JYX

You may contact me via email at melvina.carpenter@yahoo.com for speaking engagements. Please follow me on:
www.facebook.com/melvinacarpenterbooks,
www.instagram.com/melvinacarpentersbooks, and
www.twitter.com/mcarpentersbooks.

All of my books are available at all major retailers online. However, please follow me at www.amazon.com/author/melvinacarpenter to be updated on future titles. Also, if you enjoyed "Single, Pregnant and Preaching", stay tuned because another Christian love novel is on the way. Don't forget to follow me at www.amazon.com/author/melvinacarpenter.

www.amazon.com/author/melvinacarpenter

About the Book...

This book was written to simply answer the questions that I'm constantly asked via telephone or on social media sites. Many people want to know, how I wrote and published five books in three years. This book gives you a step-by-step process as to how I did it, what companies I utilized, what was easy and difficult for me. I am not an expert. This is however, my story of how things came together for me. I have shared this information with other authors and they have been successful by following these steps. I hope that you will be too! Happy writing.

About the Author...

Melvina L. Carpenter is a native of Huger, SC but currently resides in Summerville, SC. She has a Bachelor of Science degree from Claflin University in, Orangeburg, SC and a Master of Divinity from Liberty University in Lynchburg, VA. She enjoys preaching, singing, cosmetology and writing. She, along with her husband, Minister Willie Carpenter and their five children attend True Light Healing & Deliverance Ministries. There, she is the Prophetess and an Elder. She travels across the country preaching to women of every aspect the Gospel of Jesus Christ and his saving grace. She has authored several other titles. Please visit her at www.amazon.com/author/melvinacarpenter for information on book signing events and upcoming titles.